The 2 O O O Commemorative Stamp Yearbook

OTHER BOOKS FROM THE UNITED STATES POSTAL SERVICE

1999 Commemorative Stamp Yearbook

Postal Service Guide to U.S. Stamps

TWENTY-SIXTH EDITION
TWENTY-SEVENTH EDITION

The 2 ○ ○ ○ Commemorative Stamp Yearbook

UNITED STATES
POSTAL SERVICE ®

HarperResource
A Division of HarperCollins Publishers

Library of Congress Cataloging-in-Publication Data
Has been applied for.
Available upon request.
ISBN: 0-06-019896-6

**Year of the Dragon:
Lunar New Year**

**Patricia Roberts
Harris:
Black Heritage**

**U.S. Navy
Submarines**

Washington, DC
December 27, 1999

San Francisco, CA
January 6, 2000

Washington, DC
January 27, 2000

Groton, CT
March 27, 2000

Carl Herrman
Designer
Art Director

Clarence Lee
Illustrator
Designer

Photograph:
David Valdez/
Courtesy Department
of Housing and Urban
Development

Jim Griffiths
Illustrator

Terrence W. McCaffrey
U.S. Postal Service
Art Director

Carl Herrman
Designer
Art Director

Howard Paine
Designer
Art Director

Pacific Coast Rain Forest: Nature of America	**Louise Nevelson**	**Edwin Powell Hubble**	**American Samoa**
Seattle, WA March 29, 2000	New York, NY April 6, 2000	Greenbelt, MD April 10, 2000	Pago Pago, AS April 17, 2000
John D. Dawson Illustrator	Photographs: **Jerry L. Thompson**	Images: **Space Telescope Science Institute**	**Herb Kawainui Kāne** Illustrator
Ethel Kessler Designer Art Director	**Pace Wildenstein Gallery** **Whitney Museum of American Art**	**Phil Jordan** Designer Art Director	**Howard Paine** Designer Art Director
	Ethel Kessler Designer Art Director		

IN FOREST

SECOND IN A SERIES

A M E R I C A

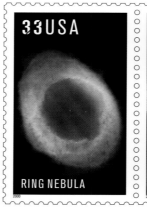

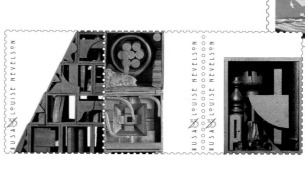

Washington, DC
April 24, 2000

Phoenix, AZ
April 26, 2000

Washington, DC
May 3, 2000

Spokane, WA
May 5, 2000

Los Angeles, CA
May 10, 2000

Photograph:
Michael Freeman

Ed Wleczyk
Warner Bros.
Illustrator
Designer

Photographs:
York: **Family Photo**
Hines: **U.S. Signal
Corps**/Courtesy
National Archives
Bradley: **U.S. Army**
Murphy: **AP/Wide
World**

Photograph:
David Madison

Greg Berger
Illustrator
Designer

Ethel Kessler
Designer
Art Director

Frank Espinosa
Warner Bros.
Character Art

Richard Sheaff
Designer
Art Director

Ethel Kessler
Art Director

Brenda Guttman
Warner Bros.
Concept

Phil Jordan
Designer
Art Director

Terrence W. McCaffrey
U.S. Postal Service
Art Director

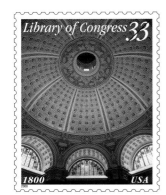

Youth Team Sports	**The Stars and Stripes: Classic Collection**	**Legends of Baseball: Classic Collection**	**Stampin' The Future™**	**California Statehood**
Lake Buena Vista, FL May 27, 2000	Baltimore, MD June 14, 2000	Atlanta, GA July 6, 2000	Anaheim, CA July 13, 2000	Sacramento, CA September 8, 2000
Photographs: **William R. Sallaz/** Sports Illustrated **Mike Powell**/Allsport **Zoran Milich** **Bob Wickley/** SuperStock, Inc. **Derry Noyes** Designer Art Director	**Richard Sheaff** Designer Art Director	**Joseph Saffold** Illustrator **Phil Jordan** Designer Art Director	**Zachary Canter** **Morgan Hill** **Sarah Lipsey** **Ashley Young** Illustrators **Richard Sheaff** Designer Art Director	Photograph: **Art Wolfe** **Carl Herrman** Designer Art Director

Edward G. Robinson: Legends of Hollywood

Deep Sea Creatures

Thomas Wolfe: Literary Arts

The White House

Burbank, CA
September 14, 2000

Monterey, CA
October 2, 2000

Asheville, NC
October 3, 2000

Washington, DC

Drew Struzan
Illustrator

Photographs:
Bruce H. Robison
Laurence P. Madin

Michael J. Deas
Illustrator

Photograph:
Patricia Fisher

Howard Paine
Designer
Art Director

Greg Berger
Designer

Phil Jordan
Designer
Art Director

Derry Noyes
Designer
Art Director

Ethel Kessler
Art Director

Behind the Scenes

Creating a postage stamp involves much more than choosing an image to illustrate a subject; it requires a strong sense of design and a mastery of techniques that are needed to produce a small, unique work of art. To meet this challenge, the commemorative stamp program of the U.S. Postal Service relies on the talents of a select group of artists, designers, and art directors who work behind the scenes to bring the public a collection of meaningful and visually striking stamps.

From undersea creatures to Hollywood legends, most of the subjects that appear on U.S. stamps and stamped cards are suggested by the public. The task of considering 50,000 letters, all brimming with ideas for stamps, falls to the Citizens' Stamp Advisory Committee (CSAC), which meets four times a year in Washington, D.C., to recommend to the Postmaster General the subjects that will appear on U.S. postage. Drawn from many walks of life, the members of CSAC are charged with selecting a combination of stamp subjects that must be interesting as well as educational. The task is formidable, but the members' range and depth of knowledge, their commitment to the public, and their personal interest in philately all ensure healthy debate and an exciting stamp program each year.

Suggestions are reviewed first by CSAC's subject subcommittee. At each quarterly meeting, the members of this subcommittee spend hours evaluating proposals, ever mindful of their unique and important responsibility. Stamp proposals, which often recommend people as stamp subjects, are an inspiring testament to the sheer number of Americans whose words, works, and very lives have shaped our nation. When considering whether to honor a person with a stamp, CSAC is bound by particular criteria to ensure that the importance of that individual has withstood the test of time. For example, no living person may be honored on U.S. postage, and with the exception of American presidents, only an individual who has been deceased for ten years may be considered for a stamp. The subjects for 2000 include a fascinating selection of men and women: four distinguished soldiers, a Cabinet member, an actor, an artist, a novelist, an astronomer, and 20 legendary baseball players.

After a stamp subject has been selected, new questions arise: How should a stamp portray a subject? Will the picture on the stamp be a painting or a photograph? To resolve these issues, art directors for the Postal Service bring their tremendous wealth of knowledge to the stamp development process, researching each subject thoroughly and considering a vast range of design options.

For several stamps each year, an original illustration is often the best way to express a subject. With the Adoption stamp, for example, illustrator Greg Berger took a conceptual approach that evokes the innocence of a child's drawing. Also for 2000, renowned poster artist Drew Struzan depicted Hollywood legend Edward G. Robinson in his own inimitable style. Some of this year's subjects, however, were best represented by photographs. The Deep Sea Creatures stamps are

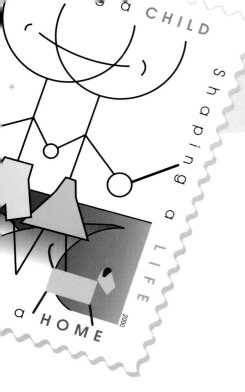

From first sketch to final art, creating a stamp presents many challenges. For each of the five different stamps in the U.S. Navy Submarines prestige booklet, for example, noted marine artist Jim Griffiths had to achieve the highest degree of accuracy. He also had to consider the overall composition—how all five stamps would look as a group. Some of his preliminary sub art appears on these two pages.

eye-catching views of rarely seen undersea life, and photographs on the stamps commemorating California statehood and the Library of Congress bicentennial successfully convey the grandeur of their subjects, even at the size of postage stamps.

Work small; think big: That's the challenge of creating art for a postage stamp. An artist must portray an important subject at a small scale without diminishing the subject's integrity or the details of the image itself. Creating a stamp is a daunting process even for experienced graphic designers, and some of the nation's most skilled illustrators may have to revise their work several times to produce art that holds up well at stamp size. Because Postal Service art directors understand what's required, they frequently work two to three years in advance, selecting artists who have command of particular subjects and who can learn to "work small."

Thousands of American children faced this challenge in the Stampin' The Future™ competition. Charged with illustrating their visions of the 21st century, youngsters from the U.S. and more than 25 other countries submitted designs to their nations' postal services. The four winning U.S. entries appear on a block of four colorful stamps this year.

With some subjects, designers face the added challenge of creating a complete, well-composed pane of stamps that stands as a work of art in its own right. John D. Dawson's painting of the Pacific

Coast Rain Forest, for instance, is full of detail and beauty; it also includes ten stamps, each of which remains an individual work of art when removed from the stamp pane. Such considerations, which are so atypical in many other areas of graphic design, are a regular part of stamp development.

At various points in the design process, art directors make formal presentations to CSAC's design subcommittee. The art directors may show several versions of proposed art for each subject, demonstrating the impressive range of approaches they consider when they develop their designs. After viewing a presentation, the subcommittee sometimes decides to send art back to the artist for revision, along with many helpful comments and suggestions. For a design to be approved, a majority of the subcommittee must vote in favor of it; the design must also receive a majority vote when all of CSAC convenes on the second day of the quarterly meeting. If approved by the full committee, the design goes to the Postmaster General for approval—and later appears in post offices across the country.

The stamps included in the *2000 Commemorative Stamp Yearbook* are the result of this thorough creative process. Each design benefits from the suggestions of a great many people who are intent upon crafting a superlative stamp. Whether for mail use or for collecting, a stamp begins with the public, and in the end it ultimately returns to the public as a small but precious example of the best America has to offer.

YEAR 2000

To many people, the year 2000 always seemed a distant symbol of far-flung tomorrows, a source of anticipation and fanciful speculation. But then the year itself arrived, and we suddenly found ourselves in the future.

Although each nation observed the arrival of the year 2000 in its own unique way, the result was a celebration on a truly global scale. As the new year swept westward and clocks struck midnight in each time zone, spectacular performances and cultural exhibitions awed audiences; in the world's great cities, dazzling displays of fireworks lit up the skies. Fears of possible Y2K computer glitches faded as the year began with no major technical problems, and the world watched unforgettable scenes from across the planet as the sun rose on a long-awaited January morning.

To commemorate the year 2000, the U.S. Postal Service presents a stamp that rings in the new with a distinctly American icon. This celebratory baby, drawn by renowned illustrator J. C. Leyendecker (1874-1951), originally appeared on the cover of the January 2, 1937, edition of *The Saturday Evening Post.* Leyendecker's New Year's babies decorated the covers of the magazine for nearly 40 years, and he contributed more than 300 covers overall during his career. This New Year's baby is a reminder of the celebrations that began the year 2000 with idealism and renewed hope.

YEAR OF THE DRAGON LUNAR NEW YEAR

The colorful Year of the Dragon stamp is the eighth of twelve stamps to be issued in the Lunar New Year series. Honoring the centuries-old Chinese lunar calendar, this series began in 1992 with the advocacy and support of the Organization of Chinese Americans. The Lunar New Year is celebrated not only by people of Chinese descent but also by Koreans, Vietnamese, Tibetans, and Mongolians.

The dragon is a traditional Chinese symbol with complex associations, including power, nobility, and good luck. Because of their sense of self-assurance, people who are born in the Year of the Dragon (for example, 1940, 1952, 1964, 1976, or 1988) can be strong-willed, but they are also natural leaders who enjoy especially good fortune. So says tradition.

The Chinese New Year, also called the Spring Festival, is a time for displaying fruits, flowers, and other symbols of abundance. Greetings and well-wishes,

typically written in black characters on red paper, are placed in windows and doors—a tradition with an ancient history. On New Year's Eve, families venerate ancestors and enjoy feasts consisting of special foods. The next day they gather with friends for public celebrations. Amid firecrackers and noisemakers, revelers and costumed participants fill the streets, and spectators may witness the performance of the traditional dragon dance. A dragon—sometimes more than 100 feet long and cast in many colors, including brilliant shades of gold, green, blue, and red—is paraded through the streets to the sounds of pounding drums and crashing cymbals.

In San Francisco's Chinatown, New Year's festivities include a dragon dance (far left), a traditional ceremony (left), and a parade (above).

PATRICIA ROBERTS HARRIS

A career including scholastic excellence, social activism, teaching, private practice, and government service led to the creation of this stamp honoring Patricia Roberts Harris.

Born May 31, 1924, in Mattoon, Illinois, Patricia Roberts was the daughter of a teacher and a Pullman car waiter. In 1945, she graduated *summa cum laude* from Howard University in Washington, D.C., where she had been active in protests against civil rights abuses in the then still segregated nation's capital. Over the next several years, she served as assistant director at the American Council on Human Rights, married attorney William Beasley Harris, and graduated from George Washington University National Law Center.

Mrs. Harris was a trial attorney at the Department of Justice and a professor at Howard University School of Law in the early 1960s. Then, in 1965, President Lyndon Johnson named her ambassador to Luxembourg—the first African-American woman to hold such a post. In 1969, she became the first woman to serve as dean of Howard University School of Law. During the 1960s and '70s, she served on the executive board of the NAACP Legal Defense Fund, became a partner in a prestigious D.C. law firm, and taught at George Washington University National Law Center.

President Jimmy Carter made Mrs. Harris a member of his Cabinet, naming her Secretary of Housing and Urban Development in 1977 and Secretary of Health, Education and Welfare in 1979. He later said she "was a fine lady and a fine Cabinet officer, sensitive to the needs of others and an able administrator....an inspiration to me and to everyone who knew her."

At left, Patricia Roberts Harris listens to reporters' questions at the 1980 White House Conference on Families. On the opposite page (background) and below, Harris confers with President Jimmy Carter. In the bottom photograph, she stands beside President Lyndon Johnson during 1965 commencement activities at Howard University in Washington, D.C.

USS *Salt Lake City*, a *Los Angeles* class attack submarine, cruises near San Diego, California. A submarine commander (inset, center) uses a periscope to scan the surface in World War II. For their actions during that war, seven submariners received the Medal of Honor (opposite, lower right). *Gato* class subs, such as USS *Harder* (opposite, bottom), served gallantly in World War II.

U.S. NAVY SUBMARINES

One century ago the U.S. Navy purchased its first submarine after a successful trial run of the 54-foot USS *Holland*. This vessel, which was driven by an internal combustion engine on the surface, switched to a battery-powered electric motor when diving.

During the final trial the USS *Holland* submerged in 12 seconds, ran a straight course at six knots for ten minutes, headed back toward her starting point, and resurfaced. Named for her inventor, John P. Holland, the warship had a crew of six plus the skipper.

An earlier, unsuccessful attempt at submarine warfare involved a round vessel named *Turtle*. It was designed during the American Revolution by a Connecticut patriot, David Bushnell. Operated by one man using cranks and pedals, *Turtle* was supposed to float on the surface, submerge beside a British ship, and place a mine on the hull of the other vessel.

Some 25 years later Robert Fulton tried to sell his *Nautilus*, a four-man, hand-cranked submarine equipped with a sail for traveling on the surface. He contacted both France and England, who were then at war, but neither was interested.

During the Civil War, the Confederacy's *H.L. Hunley*, constructed from a boiler and manned by a crew of eight, destroyed the USS *Housatonic* in a surface attack and then sank on her return to Charleston.

After *Holland*, sub designers not only made improvements that increased the range of their vessels but also introduced diesel engines. Submarines would play a larger, deadlier role in naval conflict. In World War I, for example, the German Navy used its U-boats so effectively that they threatened to cut the supply lines between North America and Europe. The sinking of the British liner RMS *Lusitania* by a German U-boat on May 7, 1915, was one of the catalysts that helped bring the United States into World War I.

The 307-foot *Gato* class subs, armed with six torpedo tubes forward and four astern, were among the most important submarine designs of World War II. To help make up for the many surface ships lost in Japan's attack on Pearl Harbor, the U.S. Navy relied heavily on its submarines; despite early problems with faulty torpedoes, the subs fought fiercely and had much success. Although they represented only 1.6 percent of the entire U.S. Navy, submarines sank a third of Japan's Navy and nearly two-thirds of its merchant marine. They also rescued 380 downed U.S. Navy pilots and many Army pilots, often under enemy fire. Seven World War II submariners received the Medal of Honor for exceptional bravery.

After the war, many innovations were made in sub design, and perhaps the most important was the introduction of nuclear power.

In the mid-1970s, the 362-foot *Los Angeles* class nuclear attack submarines began patrolling the world's oceans. Manned by highly skilled officers and crews, our *Ohio* class ballistic missile submarines have the ability to launch Trident missiles with deadly accuracy over great distances—an imposing deterrent to possible military aggression.

PACIFIC COAST RAIN FOREST

SECOND IN A SERIES

N A T U R E   O F   A M E R I C A

22

PACIFIC COAST RAIN FOREST

North America's Pacific coast is the setting for one of the largest temperate rain forests in the world. Extending from northern California to Alaska, this remarkable ecosystem is made up of numerous kinds of flora and fauna. Several of these species are shown on the Pacific Coast Rain Forest stamp pane, second in the Nature of America™ educational series.

Occupying a relatively narrow strip of land between the Pacific Ocean and the mountains to the east, the rain forest is as much as 30 miles wide in some places. Its average annual precipitation ranges from 80 to 160 inches, and the air temperature seldom drops below freezing or tops 80°F. The moderate climate and plentiful rainfall contribute to the forest's accumulation of biomass, or organic material, ranked as the highest in the world at 500 tons per acre.

Majestic conifers, including the Sitka spruce and the western hemlock, reach 200 feet or more in height here. Among the largest trees in North America, they form a dense canopy, greatly reducing the amount of sunlight reaching the forest floor. Hanging from their branches or growing on the ground below them are various mosses, ferns, shrubs, lichens, and flowers.

This thick vegetation provides a welcome habitat for birds, mammals, and reptiles. In fact, bird-watchers often hear rather than see the many birds who dwell among the trees and dense ground cover.

As shown on the stamp pane, the harlequin duck, American dipper, and winter wren are among the forest's numerous species of birds. Other creatures include the Roosevelt elk, Douglas squirrel, Pacific giant salamander, rough-skinned newt, tailed frog, western tiger swallowtail, snail-eating ground beetle, and banana slug. Also shown are the cutthroat trout and chinook salmon, just two of several kinds of fish that swim in the rivers and streams. The dwarf Oregongrape, deer fern, foliose lichen, and stair-step moss are some of the many plants that grow here. Information on the back of the pane identifies all of the illustrated species.

LOUISE NEVELSON

Louise Nevelson (née Berliawsky) arrived in the United States in 1905, a young emigrant from Kiev, Russia. After her marriage at age 20 to Charles Nevelson, the tall, flamboyant young woman moved from Rockland, Maine, to New York City, where she studied voice, drawing, and acting. In 1931 she went to Munich, Germany, to study with noted painter Hans Hofmann.

In her first solo exhibition, at New York's Nierendorf Gallery in 1941, Nevelson displayed clay and plaster sculptures as well as paintings. In the 1950s, the artist began working with "found wood"—discarded furniture, picture frames, and balustrades, for example—that she scavenged from city sidewalks. It was free and available, and she liked the medium: "Wood was the thing I could communicate with almost spontaneously and get what I was looking for....it's very alive." Nevelson began to enclose her sculptures in wooden boxes and frequently reused pieces from her previous works to achieve new effects and compositions.

The photograph above shows Louise Nevelson's 1964 sculpture, *Silent Music I.* At left, the artist poses for Arnold Newman in a 1980 photograph taken at the Whitney Museum's Nevelson retrospective in New York.

Large steel sculptures from Nevelson's later period were commissioned by Princeton University, the James A. Byrne Federal Courthouse in Philadelphia, and others; seven of her metal sculptures were placed near New York's Wall Street in an area now called Louise Nevelson Plaza. Among the many tributes she received were the American Academy of Arts and Letters Gold Medal and a National Medal of Arts from President Ronald Reagan.

The U.S. Postal Service honors Louise Nevelson with stamps featuring details of five of her works: *Silent Music I, Royal Tide I, Black Chord, Nightsphere-Light,* and *Dawn's Wedding Chapel I.*

Edwin P. Hubble

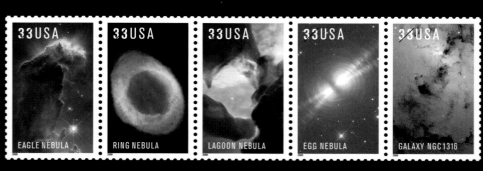

33 USA	33 USA	33 USA	33 USA	33 USA
EAGLE NEBULA	RING NEBULA	LAGOON NEBULA	EGG NEBULA	GALAXY NGC 1316

Edwin Powell Hubble, eminent American astronomer, forever changed humanity's understanding of the universe.

Born in 1889 in Marshfield, Missouri, Hubble attended the University of Chicago and studied law at Oxford as a Rhodes scholar. He passed the bar exam, but his passion was astronomy. As a graduate student at the University of Chicago, Hubble conducted research at the university's Yerkes Observatory in Wisconsin and earned his Ph.D. in astronomy in 1917. After serving in World War I, he began his groundbreaking work at Mount Wilson Observatory near Pasadena, California.

Hubble determined through his work at Mount Wilson that other galaxies exist outside of our own Milky Way and are receding from it. He also found that the more distant a galaxy is from the Earth, the faster it appears to move away. Known as Hubble's Law, this discovery provided the foundation for what some consider the most revolutionary theory of the century: the big bang theory of the creation and evolution of the expanding universe. Hubble also classified galaxies, grouping them by size and shape—a system still in use today.

The legacy of Edwin Powell Hubble, who died in 1953, is well represented by the Hubble Space Telescope. Deployed from the space shuttle _Discovery_ in April 1990, the

Hubble is the largest and most complex astronomical observatory ever placed in orbit. It travels five miles per second some 380 miles above the planet, where it can provide clearer images than Earth-based astronomical tools.

The Hubble has imaged astronomical objects hundreds of thousands of times, peering at nebulas (interstellar clouds of gas and dust) and giving scientists new insight into truly cosmic phenomena. Whether showing us the last gasps of dying stars, the creation of new stars, or the aftermath of colliding galaxies, the Hubble Space Telescope has continued the tradition of its namesake, providing major clues to the mysteries of our universe.

AMERICAN SAMOA

In 2000, American Samoans celebrate one hundred years of political affiliation with the United States.

Located more than 2,000 miles southwest of Hawaii, the five islands and two atolls of American Samoa have a total land area of about 76 square miles. The islands of Tutuila and Aunuu were ceded to the United States in April 1900 by local Samoan chiefs known as *matai*, and in 1904 the king and the chiefs of the Manua Islands ceded nearby Tau, Ofu, and Olosega. Rose Atoll was also part of the 1904 agreement. Swains Island became part of American Samoa in 1925.

For the approximately 59,000 people who live on these beautiful islands, the *aiga*—extended family—is a vital institution, with family pride an important element of life. Although residents are proud to be considered American nationals, they are also conscious of *fa'a Samoa*—the Samoan way—a commitment to traditional heritage and culture. As a result, the Samoan language continues to thrive alongside English, and most people are fluent in both.

Tuna canning is the chief industry in American Samoa. The government is another major employer, providing jobs for a large number of residents, particularly in Pago Pago, the capital city. Located on the island of Tutuila, Pago Pago is known for having one of the best harbors in the South Pacific.

American Samoa's tropical climate attracts thousands of tourists each year. Visitors encounter not only volcanic peaks, lush vegetation, and a dramatic coastline but also a friendly and welcoming combination of American and distinctly Polynesian culture.

In shallow waters offshore, a Samoan harvests the bounty of the ocean (above). Traditional costumes (right) highlight celebrations in American Samoa. Pago Pago's harbor (opposite), one of the best in the South Pacific, welcomes visitors from around the world. *Fa'a Samoa*—the Samoan way—still thrives on these beautiful islands (inset, opposite).

KNOWLEDGE COMES BVT WISDOM LINGERS

THE DE VINNE PRESS

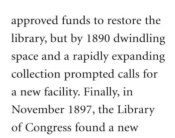

In 1800, President John Adams approved an act of Congress that appropriated $5,000 to establish a library consisting of "such books as may be necessary for the use of Congress." Since then, the Library of Congress has grown from its modest beginnings to become a peerless resource for all Americans.

The Library of Congress began as a collection of 740 books and three maps housed in the U.S. Capitol Building. After British troops burned the Capitol in 1814, Thomas Jefferson offered his personal library as a replacement, declaring that there is "no subject to which a Member of Congress may not have occasion to refer." In 1815, Congress accepted his offer and paid him $23,950 for 6,487 books, laying a great foundation for a broad-based national library.

In 1851, a fire destroyed nearly two-thirds of the library's collection, which by then numbered some 55,000 books. Congress approved funds to restore the library, but by 1890 dwindling space and a rapidly expanding collection prompted calls for a new facility. Finally, in November 1897, the Library of Congress found a new home on Capitol Hill: a magnificent Italian Renaissance structure that is now known as the Jefferson Building.

Today, the Library of Congress also comprises the Adams and Madison Buildings, and its collection of nearly 119 million items includes films, photographs, prints, maps, sound recordings, musical scores, and digital materials. It is the world's largest library and the nation's oldest federal cultural institution, as well as an enduring reminder of the importance of free access to information in a democratic society.

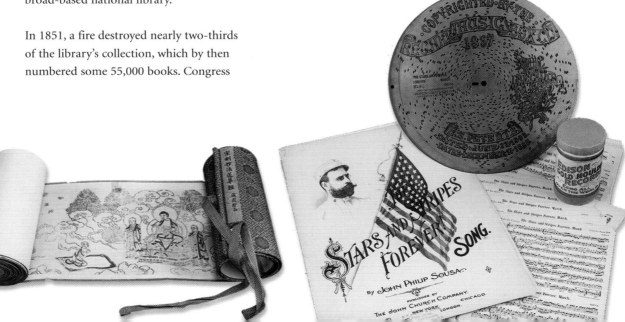

Wile E. Coyote & Road Runner

The fourth issuance in the U.S. Postal Service's Looney Tunes series pays tribute to Wile E. Coyote and Road Runner, two of America's favorite cartoon characters.

The two first appeared together in "Fast and Furry-ous," a short animated film directed by Chuck Jones. Based on a story by Michael Maltese, the cartoon showed Wile E. Coyote using 11 different methods to try to catch the elusive Road Runner. All of his attempts failed, but he would get to try again and again: The popular duo appeared in a second cartoon, "Beep Beep," and went on to star in more than 40 animated shorts.

In every cartoon, Wile E. Coyote is unshakable in his belief that he can catch the freewheeling Road Runner. Of course, he never will, and the audience always knows he won't. The question is, how will Wile E. Coyote fail?

What latest product from the Acme Company will he try next? How will the unflappable Road Runner get away from him?

All of the stories follow several tenets established by director Chuck Jones: The setting is a desert in the American Southwest; there is no dialogue—just Road Runner's cheerful signature call of "Beep! Beep!"; Road Runner always stays on the road; Wile E. Coyote causes his own mishaps but quickly bounces back; the two characters are always introduced with fanciful scientific names (*Carnivorous vulgaris* and *Accelerati incredibulis*, for example); and the audience can't help but feel sympathy for Wile E. Coyote—a lovable, comic antihero.

With this colorful stamp, the United States Postal Service and Warner Bros. bring Wile E. Coyote and Road Runner together once more.

John L. Hines • Omar N. Bradley • Alvin C. York • Audie L. Murphy

The Distinguished Soldiers stamp pane honors four American men famous for their leadership and exceptional valor. Sgt. Alvin C. York and Gen. John L. Hines served in World War I, and Lt. Audie L. Murphy and Gen. Omar N. Bradley served in World War II.

One of 11 children, **Sgt. Alvin C. York** was born in 1887 in Pall Mall, Tennessee. He had little formal education, but he knew a great deal about guns and how to use them: York became a skilled marksman while out hunting game to help feed his family.

On October 8, 1918, serving with the American Expeditionary Forces (A.E.F.) in France, Alvin York captured 132 Germans and silenced several machine guns. For his heroism he received the Medal of Honor,

a promotion to sergeant, and great international fame. After declining numerous endorsement offers, York went home to Tennessee and pursued his various philanthropic interests. A film adaptation of his life story, *Sergeant York*, was made in 1941 and starred Gary Cooper.

Gen. John L. Hines was born in 1868 in White Sulphur Springs, West Virginia, and graduated from the U.S. Military Academy in 1891. He served in the Spanish-American War in 1898 and the Philippine Insurrection of 1901.

After the United States entered World War I, Gen. John J. Pershing assigned Hines to the A.E.F. in France, where he began a meteoric rise in rank. In 16 months he progressed from major to major general, and in

1924—just six years following the armistice—he succeeded General Pershing as Army Chief of Staff.

Gen. Omar N. Bradley, born in 1893 in Clark, Missouri, received his military education at the U.S. Military Academy, from which he graduated in 1915. Throughout his many postings Bradley demonstrated his abilities as a tactician and an administrator; he was also a proven leader who showed concern for the men in his command.

During World War II, General Bradley led the First Army during the Allied landing at Normandy in June 1944. A few months later he took command of the Twelfth Army Group—at 1.3 million strong, the largest American field command in history. At war's end, Bradley

headed the Veterans Administration and then became Army Chief of Staff in 1948 and the first chairman of the Joint Chiefs of Staff in 1949. He earned his fifth star in 1950.

The most decorated American combat soldier of World War II was **Lt. Audie L. Murphy**, the son of a Texas sharecropper.

Murphy first saw action in the invasion of Sicily. In January 1945, he mounted a burning tank destroyer, and firing its machine gun at enemy troops, he stemmed their attack. He received the Medal of Honor and numerous other commendations for his bravery. After the war Murphy embarked on a career in the movies, even playing himself in *To Hell and Back* (1955).

SUMMER SPORTS

With its warm weather and long hours of daylight, summer is a great time to attend, watch, or participate in a wide variety of sporting events. Among the most popular events of the season are track-and-field competitions, invigorating athletic activities that inspired the design for the 2000 Summer Sports stamp.

Taken by noted sports photographer David Madison, the picture used for the stamp design conveys the swift pace of a summer track event. As the runners raced past, the camera captured only the blur of their fast-moving legs.

Not all summer sports involve competition, however. You also don't have to be a track-and-field star or a decathlon champion to participate in them. All you have to do is take advantage of the numerous outdoor opportunities that the season offers. Many summer sports enthusiasts, in fact, are people who don't feel that they need to be superathletes. They just enjoy getting out of the house to go for a run or to swim a few laps. They want to ride their bikes, hike in the hills, or toss Frisbees back and forth with their friends. Some people like to spend time shooting baskets, using hoops attached to their garages or playing on basketball courts at nearby gyms or parks.

Community park and recreation programs offer plenty of summer sports opportunities for children and adults. Many of them also provide trained coaches who encourage and teach athletic activities designed to improve physical fitness—and perhaps the quality of life as well.

In fast-paced summer sports action, a bicyclist (opposite) becomes a blur of color; an eight-oared shell (below) glides swiftly through the water.

ADOPTION

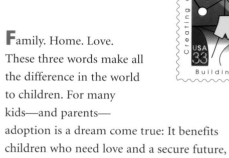

Opposite: The love of family members signals the start of a bright new day for many youngsters, and a nurturing environment brings a smile to even the smallest face.

Family. Home. Love. These three words make all the difference in the world to children. For many kids—and parents— adoption is a dream come true: It benefits children who need love and a secure future, and it gives parents a golden opportunity to share their love with a youngster.

Continuing its efforts to raise awareness about important social issues, the U.S. Postal Service joins the Dave Thomas Foundation for Adoption in calling attention to the beneficial role adoption can play in so many lives. Dave Thomas, founder of Wendy's International, Inc., was adopted as a child, and in 1992 he established a not-for-profit foundation to help make adoption more available. His foundation works to increase awareness about children awaiting adoption, lends support to other charitable groups, and provides useful guides for adoptive parents.

Each year some 120,000 infants and older children are adopted in the United States. Adoption occurs in a number of different ways. In 1992, the last year for which total adoption statistics are available, 42 percent of all adoptions were by relatives or step-parents; around 37 percent were adoptions completed in the U.S. through private agencies or independent practitioners; about 15 percent were adoptions of foster-care children through public agencies; and 5 percent were adoptions of children from other countries.

Children will benefit from the support and understanding of caring parents regardless of how they are adopted. With encouragement, adoptive parents can obtain the guidance they need to open their hearts and homes to youngsters who deserve love and a sense of belonging.

Building a HOME

YOUTH *team* sports

Basketball, football, soccer, and baseball are team sports very popular with American children. Such sports promote socialization, encourage a healthy lifestyle, and provide opportunities for young people to learn cooperation and teamwork. They are also good ways for kids to have fun.

In all sports, some athletic ability and a willingness to play by the rules are required. But team sports involve something extra: Members of a team must communicate well with one another, be responsible and reliable, think in terms of group strategy, and encourage one another. These are all skills that can help young people do well on and off the field.

Doing well does not always mean winning a game. "How you play the game," it has been said, is still very important. Helping your teammates, showing respect for them and for your opponents, and learning to be gracious in defeat and in victory are all worthy goals. Receiving respect, in turn, boosts confidence and enhances self-esteem. Being part of a group means sharing goals and pursuing common interests, which are great ways to get to know people and build camaraderie. Teammates can become good friends.

Team sports offer year-round opportunities for young people. In every season of the year, children can get exercise, learn good sportsmanship skills, and now and then experience the joy of victory and the shared celebration afterward.

The Youth Team Sports stamps feature color photographs of children enjoying the action and excitement of their sports of choice.

Children participating in team sports have fun, stay fit, and learn to work and play together.

The *Stars and Stripes*

One of the world's most powerful and widely recognized symbols, the United States flag stands for our Constitution and the American way of life, our past achievements and our dreams for the future, our love of country and our responsibilities as citizens, our diversity and our unity as a nation.

The U.S. Postal Service pays tribute to the American flag and its unique history with The Stars and Stripes stamp pane.

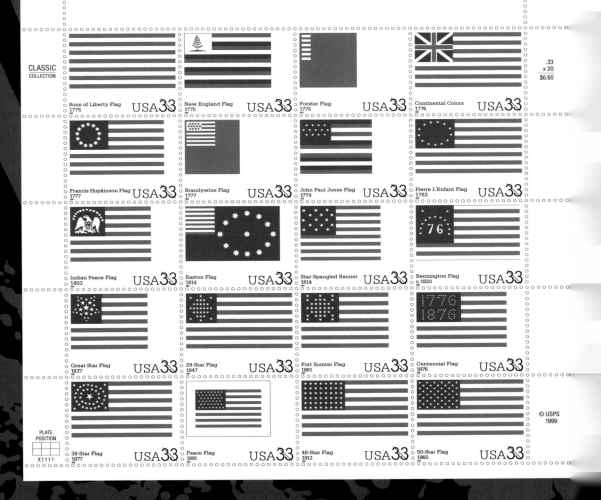

THE STARS AND STRIPES

CLASSIC
COLLECTION

.33
x 20
$6.60

Sons of Liberty Flag
1775
USA 33

New England Flag
1775
USA 33

Forster Flag
1775
USA 33

Continental Colors
1776
USA 33

Francis Hopkinson Flag
1777
USA 33

Brandywine Flag
1777
USA 33

John Paul Jones Flag
1779
USA 33

Pierre L'Enfant Flag
1783
USA 33

Indian Peace Flag
1803
USA 33

Easton Flag
1814
USA 33

Star-Spangled Banner
1814
USA 33

Bennington Flag
c.1820
USA 33

Great Star Flag
1837
USA 33

29-Star Flag
1847
USA 33

Fort Sumter Flag
1861
USA 33

Centennial Flag
1876
USA 33

© USPS
1999

PLATE
POSITION
X1111

38-Star Flag
1877
USA 33

Peace Flag
1891
USA 33

48-Star Flag
1912
USA 33

50-Star Flag
1960
USA 33

The 20 stamps that make up The Stars and Stripes pane present a variety of aesthetically interesting local, regional, and national designs. Together they trace some of the historically significant developments in the flag from colonial times to the present.

The top left corner of the stamp pane shows a flag used by the Sons of Liberty, activists in defense of American rights. This flag of 13 horizontal stripes represented the unity of the Colonies and probably inspired the stripes in Old Glory.

The British Union Jack appeared on our first national flag, in use during the early years of the Revolution. The Continental Colors sent a clear message: Until the colonists proclaimed independence in July 1776, they were fighting for their rights as subjects of King George III.

Continental Congress member Francis Hopkinson not only signed the Declaration of Independence but also wrote political satire and designed the first Stars and Stripes. The exact arrangement of the stars on Hopkinson's flag is not known; in a resolution of June 14, 1777, they were said to represent "a new constellation."

During the War of 1812, our American flag came under British fire once again. At Fort McHenry in 1814, the Star-Spangled Banner's

"broad stripes and bright stars" inspired Francis Scott Key to write words that, set to music, later became our national anthem.

In the 1860s we were at war with ourselves. The U.S. flag was flying over Charleston's Fort Sumter on April 12, 1861—when the Civil War began—and more than half a million brave men from North and South died before that very same flag was hoisted there again in 1865.

The U.S. flag is also a symbol of peace. The American government often presented the Stars and Stripes to friendly Indian nations. These "Indian Peace Flags" displayed the U.S. coat of arms and usually accompanied other gifts, including medals with the words "peace and friendship."

Using their First Amendment rights, Americans have enthusiastically pursued religious, social, and political goals and modified the flag to show commitment to country and cause. A U.S. flag bordered in white—a traditional symbol of purity and peace—was displayed at an international congress of peace in 1891.

The Flag Act of 1818 established that the U.S. flag include 13 stripes and a star for each state; when the 50th star—for Hawaii—was added on July 4, 1960, our current Stars and Stripes was born.

Dating from 1814, Fort McHenry's Star-Spangled Banner (left) now resides at the National Museum of American History in Washington, D.C. In 1999, the museum began extensive preservation work on this historic flag.

LEGENDS OF BASEBALL

This Classic Collection features 20 nominees for the Major League Baseball® All-Century Team—extraordinary men who are enshrined not only in the Hall of Fame but also in the memories of their fans.

Legends of Baseball

CLASSIC
COLLECTION

.33
x 20
$6.60

USA 33  JACKIE ROBINSON	USA 33 EDDIE COLLINS	USA 33 CHRISTY MATHEWSON	USA 33 TY COBB	USA 33 GEORGE SISLER
USA 33  ROGERS HORNSBY	USA 33  MICKEY COCHRANE	USA 33  BABE RUTH	USA 33  WALTER JOHNSON	USA 33  ROBERTO CLEMENTE
USA 33  LEFTY GROVE	USA 33  TRIS SPEAKER	USA 33  CY YOUNG	USA 33  JIMMIE FOXX	USA 33  PIE TRAYNOR
USA 33  SATCHEL PAIGE	USA 33  HONUS WAGNER	USA 33  JOSH GIBSON	USA 33  DIZZY DEAN	USA 33  LOU GEHRIG

© USPS
2000

PLATE
POSITION

X1111

The U.S. Postal Service is proud to honor these 20 legends of baseball:

Jackie Robinson (1919-1972) was voted Most Valuable Player in the National League in 1949; just two years earlier he had broken the Major League Baseball color barrier by signing with the Brooklyn Dodgers. **Rogers Hornsby** (1896-1963), the most impressive right-handed hitter in Major League Baseball, won seven batting championships, six of them with the St. Louis Cardinals. In 1931, pitcher **Lefty Grove** (1900-1975)— among the best left-handers in Major League Baseball—put together a 16-game winning streak and went 31-4 for the Philadelphia Athletics. At age 42, after two decades in the Negro Leagues, "veteran-rookie" **Satchel Paige** (1906-1982) helped pitch the Cleveland Indians to the American League pennant.

An outstanding base runner and batter, **Eddie Collins** (1887-1951) played for 25 seasons, a 20th-century record for nonpitchers. A fierce competitor at the plate and behind it, **Mickey Cochrane** (1903-1962) helped the Philadelphia Athletics win three championships. **Tris Speaker** (1888-1958) starred in center field for the Cleveland Indians, recording more career assists than any other outfielder. **Honus Wagner** (1874-1955), the Pittsburgh Pirates' star shortstop, led the National League in batting for 8 seasons and posted 15 consecutive .300 seasons.

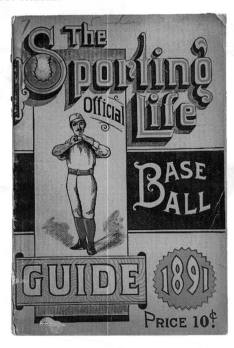

Christy Mathewson (1880-1925) pitched three shutouts in six days to help the New York Giants defeat the Philadelphia Athletics in the 1905 World Series. Before beginning his legendary career as a slugger with the New York Yankees, the celebrated **Babe Ruth** (1895-1948) pitched for the Boston Red Sox. **Cy Young** (1867-1955) was a right-handed pitcher whose record 511 wins and 749 complete games may never be topped. An incredible power hitter, **Josh Gibson** (1911-1947) ranked among the most popular players in the Negro Leagues.

Ty Cobb (1886-1961), one of the best all-around players in Major League Baseball, won 12 American League batting titles for the Detroit Tigers. Fireballer **Walter Johnson** (1887-1946) won 417 games in his 21-year career with the Washington Senators. For 12 consecutive seasons, **Jimmie Foxx** (1907-1967) hit 30 or more home runs; he led the American League in homers, hitting, and RBIs while playing for the Philadelphia Athletics in 1933. Throwing fastballs for the St. Louis Cardinals, **Dizzy Dean** (1910-1974) once held the modern single-game record for strikeouts (17).

Known as one of the true gentlemen in Major League Baseball, **George Sisler** (1893-1973) of the St. Louis Browns won two batting titles and set the record for hits in a season. The Pittsburgh Pirates' **Roberto Clemente** (1934-1972) was the first Hispanic elected to the Hall of Fame; he was known both for his superb hitting and philanthropic spirit. **Pie Traynor** (1899-1972), another skilled batsman with the Pittsburgh Pirates, ranks among the all-time best third basemen in Major League Baseball. And the "Iron Horse" **Lou Gehrig** (1903-1941), who starred at first base for the New York Yankees, set records for successive games (2,130) and career grand slams (23).

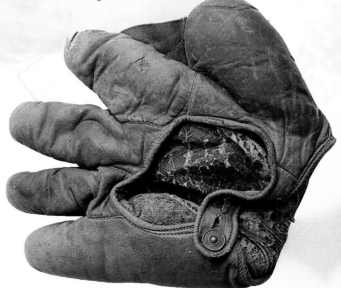

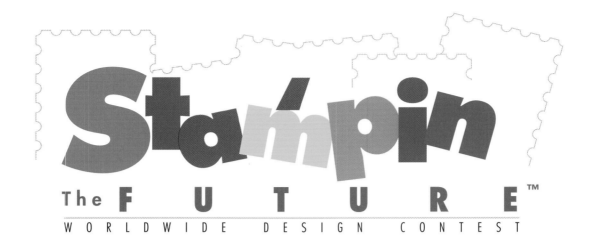

In 1998, 120,000 schoolchildren expressed their visions of the 21st century in Stampin' The Future™, a stamp art competition that was sponsored by the U.S. Postal Service.

Children 8 through 12 years old were invited by the Postal Service to create drawings based on their views of the future and to submit them through classrooms, stamp clubs, post offices, military bases, or libraries. These drawings then were judged according to originality of ideas, artistic ability, neatness and clarity, and suitability for stamp production. The winning entries became commemorative stamps.

During the first round of judging, a four-person panel—an educator, a stamp designer, an illustrator, and a comic-book editor and publisher—reviewed all of the entries and narrowed them down to 540 semifinalists. The panel then submitted its selections to the Citizens' Stamp Advisory Committee (CSAC), an independent group that ensures the integrity of the Commemorative Stamp Program; CSAC selected its favorite designs and sent them to the Postmaster General, who chose the final four.

Children in the United States were not the only ones who got to offer their visions of the future. The U.S. contest inspired similar competitions in 27 other countries, including Canada, Israel, China, Brazil, Spain, Suriname, Greece, and Iceland. For their contests, postal administrations in the other countries followed the same rules and regulations established by the U.S. Postal Service.

In 1999 many of the winning entries were exhibited at France's international stamp show in Paris. Another exhibition was held in Beijing, China, the site of the Universal Postal Congress, which meets every fifth year in a different country. In July 2000, in Anaheim, California, winners from around the world gathered at World Stamp Expo 2000™, an international philatelic exhibition hosted by the U.S. Postal Service. On exhibit were the four designs that became U.S. stamps: "Astronauts," by Zachary Canter of Kailua, Hawaii; "Children," by Sarah Lipsey of Memphis, Tennessee; "Rocket," by Morgan Hill of Montclair, New Jersey; and "Dog," by Ashley Young of Sandy, Utah.

Floating City
Singapore

Dawn Koh, Singapore

Andrew Wright, Canada

Joachim Beckers, Belgium

JERSEY

2000

Stampin' The Future contest winner
'Solar Power'

SOLAR POWER

SOLAR POWER

21

Chantal Varley-Best

2000 ©

Questa

Chantal Varley-Best,
Jersey, United Kingdom

Jonas Sampaio de Freitas – 12 anos
Piracaia/SP

Jonas Sampaio de Freitas, Brazil

Josette Saddan Aguilar Patiño, Panama

ISRAEL

יחד למאה ה-21

STAMPIN' THE FUTURE

Ortal Hasid, Israel

CALIFORNIA

STATEHOOD

Opposite (left to right): California encompasses such natural wonders as the rugged rocks along the Big Sur coastline, the bleak sandscape of Death Valley, and the waterfalls and mountains of Yosemite National Park. Above (left to right): Scenes from California's past include Hollywood circa 1905—before it became an entertainment capital—and Yosemite National Park in the early 20th century, where visitors posed with a giant "drive-through" redwood.

As California celebrates the sesquicentennial of its statehood in 2000, the United States Postal Service honors the occasion with a commemorative stamp. Featuring a scenic view by renowned nature photographer Art Wolfe, the stamp shows cliffs at the southern end of the Big Sur coastline, just south of Ragged Point.

California's road to statehood was a relatively short one. On February 2, 1848, Mexico and the United States signed a treaty ending the Mexican War, and as part of that peace treaty, Mexico agreed to cede a vast portion of the Southwest, including present-day California, to the United States. Several days earlier, on January 24, 1848, carpenter James Marshall had discovered gold at Sutter's Mill on the American River near Sacramento. The ensuing gold rush hastened the territory's admittance to the Union, and California became the 31st state on September 9, 1850.

Over the past 150 years, California has become the most populous state in the nation, counting more than 34 million residents this year. From the cosmopolitan bayside charm of San Francisco to the glitz and glamour of Los Angeles, California's cities offer something for everyone. Among those offerings are the Golden Gate Bridge and Hollywood, two of the most recognizable American icons in the world. California also boasts spectacular natural beauty. The dramatic Big Sur coastline, for example, plunges into the Pacific Ocean; towering redwoods humble visitors to Muir Woods National Monument; and the glacially carved Yosemite Valley offers days of adventure among its cliffs, waterfalls, and rock formations.

Although the gold rush has long since passed into history, people still come to the Golden State in great numbers. California leads the nation in farming and is an important center for a number of industries, including aerospace, electronics, and filmmaking. The natural beauty and exciting cities beckon to visitors, many of whom decide to stay— perhaps echoing the sentiments of forty-niners during the gold rush, whose legendary exclamation has since become the state motto: "*Eureka*—I have found it."

The many faces of Edward G. Robinson included (above, from top to bottom) a tough newspaper editor in *Five Star Final* (1931), a professional gambler in *The Cincinnati Kid* (1965), and an aged researcher in the futuristic *Soylent Green* (1973).

EDWARD G. ROBINSON

The sixth stamp in the Legends of Hollywood series honors Edward G. Robinson, whose career spanned decades to include stage, radio, television, and film roles.

Born Emanuel Goldenberg in Romania in 1893, Robinson immigrated to the United States with his family when he was a young boy. In 1913 he began a career in the theater, where he worked for many years before moving into film.

Robinson was propelled to stardom in 1931 with the title role in the film *Little Caesar,* winning praise for his performance as gangster Rico Bandello. Although he is best remembered for his classic portrayals of gangsters—including his role as Johnny Rocco in *Key Largo* (1948)—Robinson also played farmers, doctors, detectives, and even sea captains. He starred in Westerns, portrayed federal agents, and won acclaim as an insurance executive in the classic *Double Indemnity* (1944). Shortly before he died in 1973, Robinson received a special Academy Award® for lifetime achievement in films.

At right, *Kid Galahad* (1937) featured Edward G. Robinson in a memorable role as fight manager Nick Donati. Robinson starred alongside Bette Davis and Humphrey Bogart.

"If I were just a bit taller and I was a little more handsome or something like that," Robinson once said, "I could have played all the roles that I have played, and played many more…. It kept me from certain roles that I might have had, but then, it kept others from playing *my* roles, so I don't know that it's not altogether balanced."

Robinson was as versatile off the silver screen as he was on it. He had a reputation for philanthropy, and he was said to have owned one of America's finest private art collections.

Robinson (left) won praise for elevating the character of gangster Rico Bandello to the level of classical tragedy in *Little Caesar* (1931).

Licensed by Francesca Robinson Sanchez represented by Global Icons, Los Angeles, CA.
Licensed by George Sidney represented by Thomas A. White, Beverly Hills, CA.

DEEPSEA CREATURES

Darkness, cold, and high pressure characterize the deep sea, Earth's most expansive animal habitat. Life is able to exist under these conditions, but it differs significantly from that of other regions in the ocean. Among the denizens of this rarely seen world are organisms with unusual body forms and specialized mating habits; some are even bioluminescent, which means they have the ability to generate light.

The creatures depicted on these stamps dwell primarily in the mid-water range of Earth's oceans—the mesopelagic and the bathypelagic zones. Beginning approximately 100 meters (330 feet) below the surface, the mesopelagic zone extends downward almost 1,000 meters (3,300 feet). The bathypelagic zone, approximately 1,000 meters and below, is eternally dark—except for the light produced by its bioluminescent inhabitants.

Caulophryne jordani, the fanfin anglerfish, is one of more than a hundred species of deep-sea anglerfish. Most female anglerfish dangle a bioluminescent lure from the first ray of the dorsal fin. In some species, the male is much smaller than the female, does not have a lure, and lives parasitically on the body of the female.

A generic term, "sea cucumber" encompasses more than a thousand species of marine invertebrates. The species depicted on the stamp, *Enypniastes eximia,* feeds on the nutrient-rich sediment of the ocean floor and then swims to higher depths, probably to avoid bottom-dwelling predators. If another animal strikes this bioluminescent creature, the attacker gets quickly covered with a sticky, glowing substance that makes it vulnerable to its own predators.

The fangtooth, *Anoplogaster cornuta,* is a predatory fish that is found in mid-water habitats around the world. Although this fish's spiny back and large jaws give it an imposing appearance, its body usually measures only about six to eight inches long.

The general term "amphipod" describes approximately 5,000 crustaceans in a wide range of marine habitats. The species on the stamp, *Cystisoma neptunus,* can grow to a length of about six inches, making it relatively large among amphipods. Its transparent body may help protect it from predators, and the large red areas on its head are compound eyes that collect dim light.

"Medusa" is the term for the typical body form of jellyfish, free-swimming invertebrates that vary greatly in size and inhabit waters around the world. In general, these creatures occupy mid-water habitats but tend to live closer to the surface in cooler regions. The species depicted on the stamp, a bioluminescent medusa known as *Periphylla periphylla,* has been known to migrate upward at night and downward during the day.

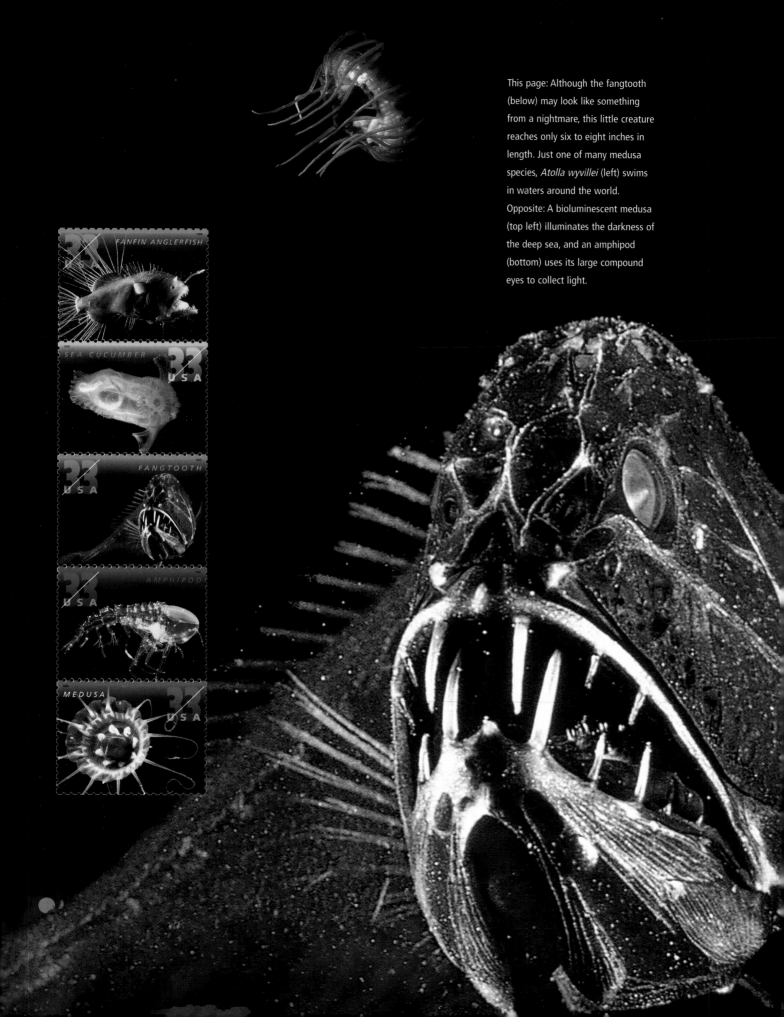

This page: Although the fangtooth (below) may look like something from a nightmare, this little creature reaches only six to eight inches in length. Just one of many medusa species, *Atolla wyvillei* (left) swims in waters around the world. Opposite: A bioluminescent medusa (top left) illuminates the darkness of the deep sea, and an amphipod (bottom) uses its large compound eyes to collect light.

FANFIN ANGLERFISH
USA
33

SEA CUCUMBER
33
USA

FANGTOOTH
33
USA

AMPHIPOD
33
USA

MEDUSA
33
USA

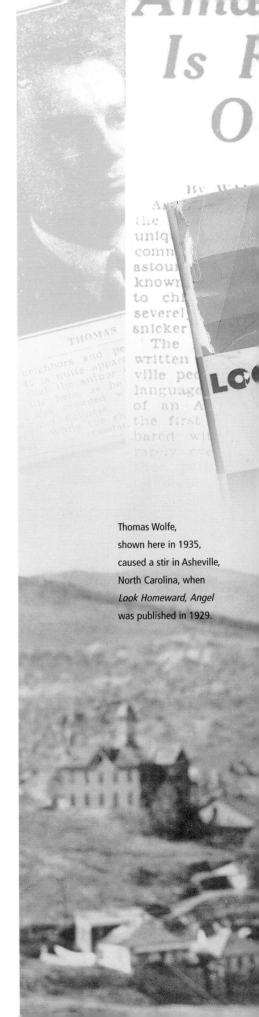

With this stamp, the U.S. Postal Service commemorates the centenary of the birth of Thomas Clayton Wolfe, one of America's great 20th-century writers.

Wolfe was born October 3, 1900, in Asheville, North Carolina, the son of a stonecutter and a boardinghouse owner. He graduated from the University of North Carolina in 1920 and continued his education at Harvard, where he received his master's degree in English in 1922.

Wolfe's first novel, *Look Homeward, Angel*, was published in 1929. An autobiographical story, *Look Homeward, Angel* followed the growth of protagonist Eugene Gant in a town called Altamont, closely modeled on Asheville. Although the novel received critical acclaim, it caused great controversy in Wolfe's hometown.

Before his untimely death in 1938 at the age of 37, Wolfe published a number of literary works. He further chronicled the life of Eugene Gant in *Of Time and the River* (1935), a sequel to *Look Homeward, Angel*. He also published numerous short stories in magazines and journals such as *The New Yorker, The New Republic*, and *The Saturday Evening Post*. One of his most powerful short novels, *I Have a Thing to Tell You,* was a criticism of Nazi Germany based on his experiences traveling in Europe. It later appeared in an expanded form in *You Can't Go Home Again*, one of Wolfe's posthumously published novels.

Thomas Wolfe approached his life and times with exuberant language and a flair for autobiographical fiction, leaving behind a body of work that richly defined his experiences as an American.

Thomas Wolfe, shown here in 1935, caused a stir in Asheville, North Carolina, when *Look Homeward, Angel* was published in 1929.

The White House

The U.S. Postal Service joins the White House in commemorating the 200th anniversary of the first residency of the White House, an enduring symbol of the American Presidency. The first occupant was John Adams, the second President of the United States. Adams and his family moved into the unfinished "President's House" in November 1800, and every President since then has lived in the Executive Mansion.

Designed by Irish-born architect James Hoban and built at a cost of $400,000, the White House is a Georgian mansion in the Palladian style. In its early stages the structure was drafty and cold, especially in the wintertime, and it lacked many conveniences. Water, for example, had to be carried to the mansion from a spring about half a mile away.

During the War of 1812 British forces occupied Washington and burned several public buildings, including the White House. The fire, in August 1814, destroyed the mansion's interior and badly damaged the exterior walls. For several months the White House remained an immense ruin. Finally, in March 1815, James Hoban was hired to rebuild the mansion, and by late 1817 President James Monroe was able to take up residency there.

Over the decades, many changes and improvements have been made. Such conveniences as running water and an indoor bathroom were installed in 1833; electric lights were added in 1891. After Theodore Roosevelt became President in 1901, he not only changed the mansion's official name to the White House but also oversaw an extensive remodeling project that expanded the family quarters and created more space for office workers. In 1948, during the administration of President Harry Truman, the building was examined and found to be structurally unsafe. It was subsequently gutted, reinforced with steel and concrete, and rebuilt within the original walls.

The White House is, of course, more than a residence for the First Family. It is also a focal point of the nation, a place to receive dignitaries and heads of state, and a museum to be viewed by the American people and visitors from abroad. The stately mansion at 1600 Pennsylvania Avenue, in the heart of the nation's capital, remains an American symbol recognized around the world.

Left: 18th-century carvings adorn the White House's north entrance. Right: In 1950, the mansion appeared on a stamp commemorating the national capital's sesquicentennial.

Photo Credits

Behind the Scenes
Pages 10-13
©2000 U.S. Postal Service

Year 2000
Pages 14-15
(all)
AP/Wide World Photos

Year of the Dragon:
Lunar New Year
Pages 16-17
(photographs)
©Carol Simowitz

Patricia Roberts Harris:
Black Heritage
Page 18
Courtesy Jimmy Carter Library

Page 19
(left)
AP/Wide World Photos
(right top)
National Archives/Courtesy PhotoAssist, Inc.
(right bottom)
©Bettmann/CORBIS

U.S. Navy Submarines
Page 20
©1987 Steve Kaufman/Yogi, Inc.

Pages 20-21
National Archives/Courtesy PhotoAssist, Inc.

Page 21
(bottom, both)
Original Prismacolor rendering
by Michael W. Wooten

Pacific Coast Rain Forest:
Nature of America
Pages 22-23
(background photograph)
©Rene Pauli/SuperStock, Inc.

Louise Nevelson
Pages 24-25
© Arnold Newman

Page 25
© Pace Wildenstein Gallery

Edwin Powell Hubble
Page 26
Image courtesy of
The Huntington Library,
San Marino, California

Page 27
(top)
Signature courtesy of
The Huntington Library,
San Marino, California
(bottom)
NASA

American Samoa
Page 28
(background)
©Anne B. Keiser
(inset)
©Kip F. Evans, Mountain & Sea Images

Page 29
(all)
©Kip F. Evans, Mountain & Sea Images

Library of Congress
Page 30
©Anne Day/Courtesy Library of Congress

Page 31
(top)
©2000 U.S. Postal Service
(bottom, all)
©Jonathan Wallen

Wile E. Coyote & Road Runner
Pages 32-33
Courtesy Warner Bros.

Distinguished Soldiers
Page 35
(top left)
National Archives/Courtesy PhotoAssist, Inc.
(top right)
National Archives/Courtesy PhotoAssist, Inc.
(middle)
National Archives/Courtesy PhotoAssist, Inc.
(bottom left)
National Archives/Courtesy PhotoAssist, Inc.
(bottom right)
U.S. Army Signal Corps Photo/Courtesy
PhotoAssist, Inc.

Summer Sports
Pages 36-37
(both)
©David Madison

Adoption

Page 38

(top)
©David M. Grossman
(bottom)
©Susie Fitzhugh
Additional artwork
©2000 U.S. Postal Service

Page 39

(bottom)
©2000 U.S. Postal Service

Youth Team Sports

Pages 40-41

(both)
©David Madison

Page 41

(top)
©DUOMO/William R. Sallaz

The Stars and Stripes: Classic Collection

Page 42-43

AP/Wide World Photos

Pages 42, 44-45

Smithsonian Institution

Legends of Baseball: Classic Collection

Pages 46-49

(all)
©USPS/Courtesy Ron Menchine Collection

Stampin' The Future™

Page 51

(all)
Courtesy U.S. Postal Service

California Statehood

Page 52

(all)
©David Muench

Page 53

(left)
©David Muench
(top left)
©Marc Wanamaker/Bison Archives
(top right)
©Bettmann/CORBIS

Edward G. Robinson: Legends of Hollywood

Page 54

(top left)
Five Star Final
©1931 Turner Entertainment Co.
All Rights Reserved. Courtesy Warner Bros.
and Turner Entertainment Co.
(middle left)
The Cincinnati Kid
©1965 Turner Entertainment Co. All Rights
Reserved. Courtesy Warner Bros. and
Turner Entertainment Co.
(bottom left)
Soylent Green
©1973 Turner Entertainment Co. All Rights
Reserved. Courtesy Warner Bros. and
Turner Entertainment Co.

Pages 54-55

Little Caesar
©1930 Turner Entertainment Co. All Rights
Reserved. Courtesy Warner Bros. and
Turner Entertainment Co.

Page 55

Kid Galahad
©1937 Turner Entertainment Co. All Rights
Reserved. Courtesy Warner Bros. and
Turner Entertainment Co.

Deep Sea Creatures

Page 56

(upper left)
©L.P. Madin, W.H.O.I.
(lower left)
©L.P. Madin, W.H.O.I.

Page 57

(top)
©Rob Sherlock/MBARI
(background)
©Bruce H. Robison/MBARI

Thomas Wolfe: Literary Arts

Pages 58-59

(all)
North Carolina Collection,
University of North Carolina Library
at Chapel Hill

Reprinted with the permission of Scribner, a
Division of Simon & Schuster from LOOK
HOMEWARD, ANGEL by Thomas Wolfe
(New York: Charles Scribner's Sons, 1929).

Reprinted with the permission of Scribner, a
Division of Simon & Schuster from OF
TIME AND THE RIVER by Thomas Wolfe
(New York: Charles Scribner's Sons, 1935).

YOU CAN'T GO HOME AGAIN reprinted
courtesy HarperCollins Publishers.

The White House

Pages 60-61

Richard Cheek, The White House

Acknowledgments

These stamps and this stamp collecting book were produced by Public Affairs and Communications, Stamp Services, United States Postal Service.

William J. Henderson
Postmaster General,
Chief Executive Officer

Deborah K. Willhite
Senior Vice President,
Government Relations and Public Policy

Azeezaly S. Jaffer
Vice President,
Public Affairs and Communications

James C. Tolbert, Jr.
Executive Director,
Stamp Services

Special thanks are extended to the following individuals for their contributions:

United States Postal Service
Terrence W. McCaffrey
Manager, Stamp Development

Kelly L. Spinks
Project Manager

HarperCollins Publishers
Megan Newman
Editorial Director,
HarperResource

Greg Chaput
Associate Editor,
HarperResource

Lucy Albanese
Design Director,
General Books Group

Roberto de Vicq de Cumptich
Art Director,
HarperResource

Kessler Design Group, Ltd.
Ethel Kessler
Art Director

Ethel Kessler and Greg Berger, *Designers*
Jon Howard, *Production*

Copywriter
Jeanne O'Neill

PhotoAssist, Inc.
Rebecca Hirsh, *Project Coordinator*
Carolinda E. Averitt, *Text Editor*
Jeff Sypeck, *Assistant Text Editor*
Victoria Cooper, Jake Flack, and
    Nick Marston, *Text Research and*
    Additional Writing
Darby O'Donnell, *Photo Research*
Jeni Sheaffer, *Rights and Permissions*

The Citizens' Stamp Advisory Committee
Dr. Virginia M. Noelke
Dr. C. Douglas Lewis
Ronald A. Robinson
Michael R. Brock
Meredith J. Davis
David Lewis Eynon
I. Michael Heyman
John M. Hotchner
Karl Malden
Philip B. Meggs
Richard F. Phelps
John Sawyer III
Irma Zandl